Love is the best journey.

Adventure awaits.

Research shows that exciting or adrenaline-filled activities create emotional bonds similar to falling in love. Studies show that people feel emotions more intensely when they experience adrenaline and have a higher heart rate.

Let these adventures together bring you even closer and create a deeper connection. Build memories that won't be easy to forget. Nothing is more important than connecting with your person.

As you embrace this journey, remember that the real adventure lies in that person you want to spend every day with. With your love, you are building something that has never been before. Sure, relationships are common, but there have never been two people quite like you, creating something like this. It can be easy to get into a rut, thinking your narrative is old news, but the truth is, you'll never arrive at fully knowing the person across from you, since both of you are always changing.

You are on this adventure together, knowing that even as you grow older, your connection can remain full of history, while also staying fresh and new. Relationships should be fun! So, here's to the never-ending enjoyment of one another, to taking risks of deeper connection and to discovering the person you are continually falling in love with.

Love is the best journey.

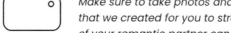

Make sure to take photos and post them on your iHeartUs app. iHeartUs is a free app for couples that we created for you to strengthen your relationship. Studies have shown that looking at photos of your romantic partner can make you feel even more connected to them.

How it works.

We have created this book to have five different types of dates, depending on the mood you're in. The five types of dates are Adventure; Chillax; Active; Nature-Oriented; and Romantic.

Teach Together

Gather a group and teach them a new skill. (Baking bread, intuitive painting, making homemade deodorant.) The goal is teamwork! The sillier the activity, the better.

We have also added some questions we call conversation starters for you to use on your date, which will help you go a little deeper or think a little more creatively about the types of questions to ask your partner.

Conversation Starters

- What's one of your hidden talents?
- What age do you feel right now and why?
- What could you give a 30 minute presentation on without preparation?

 *We did it! Bucket List Item Complete.*

After making an amazing memory, check off your bucket list item!

Try your first bucket list item.

Then post a picture and tag us on Instagram @iheartusapp!

Master Chef

A little friendly competition. Choose a recipe and have a cook-off! Set a time limit and guidelines for ingredients. Gather friends to judge who cooked it best

Conversation Starters

- If you could be on any game show, which would you choose?
- What's the most useless talent you have?
- What's something you want our family to be known for?

☐ *We did it! Bucket List Item Complete.*

Adventure

/ad'ven(t)SHər,əd'ven(t)SHər/

An unusual and exciting, typically hazardous, experience or activity.

01. Beach Trippin'

Plan a surprise road trip to the nearest beach. If a beach is too far from you, take your person to your nearest lake. If you want to take it to the next level, rent a convertible. Walk along the water's edge holding hands. Rub sunscreen on each other. Be kids again - play Frisbee, see who can build the best sandcastle, jump in on a volleyball game or try surfing.

Conversation Starters

- What was your first trip to the beach like as a child?
- Where and when was the most amazing sunset you've ever experienced?
- What is one of your best memories involving water?

☐ *We did it! Bucket List Item Complete.*

04. Surprise day trip

Plan a surprise day trip for your significant other.

Conversation Starters

- Why did you choose this place?
- Name 3 words that describe me.
- What are some places you'd like to take a day trip to in the future?

☐ *We did it! Bucket List Item Complete.*

 Make sure to take photos and post them on your iHeartUs app. iHeartUs is a free app for couples that we created for you to strengthen your relationship. Studies have shown that looking at photos of your romantic partner can make you feel even more connected to them.

02. White water river rafting

Plan a date to go white water river rafting with other couples. Definitely not the old dinner and a movie date, this is the perfect date to spice things up. Your significant other will be impressed that you came up with such an adventurous and exhilarating date. Plus, you'll be surrounded by natural beauty and romantic scenery.

Conversation Starters

- What is the most adventurous thing you've done?
- Have you ever been scared in nature? When? What happened?
- What is your favorite water sport? When did you first try it?

We did it! Bucket List Item Complete.

Make sure to take photos and post them on your iHeartUs app. iHeartUs is a free app for couples that we created for you to strengthen your relationship. Studies have shown that looking at photos of your romantic partner can make you feel even more connected to them.

Bucket List Tip

Pack your SO's favorite childhood snacks!

03. Mountain-biking

Go mountain-biking together. Don't leave them behind. Find a romantic spot to pull over and enjoy the surprise picnic you packed.

Conversation Starters

- When did you first learn to ride a bike?
- What's your scariest memory on a bike?
- What would you rather ride more? A road bike; mountain bike, motorcycle, vespa or an electric scooter? Why?

☐ *We did it! Bucket List Item Complete.*

05. Amusement Park

Amusement park date. Be kids again. Find a merry-go-round and talk about the questions below.

Conversation Starters

- Tell me your first or favorite memory at an amusement park.
- What were your favorite rides? What ride do you hate?
- What's your favorite amusement park food?

☐ *We did it! Bucket List Item Complete.*

06. Break the rules

Do something just a little naughty. Break the rules a little together. Skinny dipping, light sidewalk graffiti, sneak into a hotel pool/hot tub. Doing something you aren't supposed to can actually bring couples together. Plus, it's great for laughs and a future story.

Conversation Starters

- What was one of the worst things you did as a child?
- When was a time you were rebellious?
- What's one thing you did as a kid that you miss today?

☐ *We did it! Bucket List Item Complete.*

07. Bungee or sky-dive

Go bungee jumping or sky-diving.

Conversation Starters

- Has anyone ever saved your life?
- What are some things you want to accomplish before you die?
- What's the biggest risk you've ever taken (physically or metaphorically)?

☐ *We did it! Bucket List Item Complete.*

 Make sure to take photos and post them on your iHeartUs app. iHeartUs is a free app for couples that we created for you to strengthen your relationship. Studies have shown that looking at photos of your romantic partner can make you feel even more connected to them.

08. Rent a vespa

Rent a Vespa or electric scooters and go for a ride. Sightseeing on the back of a Vespa can be pretty romantic.

Conversation Starters

- Would you go on a cross-country road trip?
- What's the most spontaneous thing you've ever done?
- How old were you when you first drove a car or motorized vehicle? What was it like?

☐ *We did it! Bucket List Item Complete.*

09. Race Go-karts

Race Go-karts and ignite the competitive side in your partner.

**Conversation
Starters**

- What kinds of activities make you competitive?
- Would you ever want to drive a Nascar around the track for fun?
- Do you have a thirst for adventure? What type of adventure is your favorite?

☐ *We did it! Bucket List Item Complete.*

 Make sure to take photos and post them on your iHeartUs app. iHeartUs is a free app for couples that we created for you to strengthen your relationship. Studies have shown that looking at photos of your romantic partner can make you feel even more connected to them.

10. Help out together

**Volunteer at a local charity or soup kitchen together or go on a
short-term mission trip to poor villages.**

**Conversation
Starters**

- What problem in society are you passionate about helping to solve?
- When was a time you helped someone that made you feel really good?
- If you could buy a plane ticket to do volunteer work anywhere in the
  world, where would it be?

☐ *We did it! Bucket List Item Complete.*

11. Hide n seek

Play hide n seek in your house with or without clothes.

Conversation Starters

- What was one of your favorite games to play as a child?
- Where is your favorite place you've lived?
- If you could give me a tour of your hometown, where would you would take me?

☐ *We did it! Bucket List Item Complete.*

Make sure to take photos and post them on your iHeartUs app. iHeartUs is a free app for couples that we created for you to strengthen your relationship. Studies have shown that looking at photos of your romantic partner can make you feel even more connected to them.

Bucket List Tip

Spice it up with themed outfits from your favorite era! Go out in style!

12. Karaoke!

Find a karaoke bar (if one of you really don't like to sing, just go and watch to be entertained.)

Conversation Starters

- Do you like to sing? Why or why not?
- What's your favorite kind of performance to watch? Concert, theatre, musical, movie, ballet, symphony, etc.?
- What's your favorite type of art to create?

☐ *We did it! Bucket List Item Complete.*

13. Night at the casino

Plan a night at the casino. Place a bet together.

**Conversation
Starters**

- When was the first time you gambled? What was it like?
- Did you ever win something either in a casino or in a contest?
- Do you have an addictive personality? Why or why not? If you were going to be addicted to something, what would it be?

☐ *We did it! Bucket List Item Complete.*

 Make sure to take photos and post them on your iHeartUs app. iHeartUs is a free app for couples that we created for you to strengthen your relationship. Studies have shown that looking at photos of your romantic partner can make you feel even more connected to them.

14. Hot air balloon ride

Hot air balloon ride (or make a date to watch hot air balloons). If you're concerned about cost, most flights average around $90-$250.

Conversation Starters

- Are you afraid of heights?
- If you could fly in a hot air balloon over any place in the world, where/what would you want to see?
- What is something wild and crazy you have always wanted to do/experience?

☐ *We did it! Bucket List Item Complete.*

Make sure to take photos and post them on your iHeartUs app. iHeartUs is a free app for couples that we created for you to strengthen your relationship. Studies have shown that looking at photos of your romantic partner can make you feel even more connected to them.

Bucket List Tip

Why not take a instant camera with you?
Instant fun and you get to take a memory with you when you go home.

15. Horseback riding

Go horseback riding.

**Conversation
Starters**

- What is one of your favorite childhood memories with an animal?
- What exotic animal would you most like to own as a pet?
- What animal best describes your personality and why?

We did it! Bucket List Item Complete.

16. Bar-hopping

Spend a night bar-hopping.

**Conversation
Starters**

- When is the first time you got drunk? What did you drink?
- Tell me about one of your most embarrassing moments?
- What did you think was cool when you were young but don't think is cool now?

☐ *We did it! Bucket List Item Complete.*

 Make sure to take photos and post them on your iHeartUs app. iHeartUs is a free app for couples that we created for you to strengthen your relationship. Studies have shown that looking at photos of your romantic partner can make you feel even more connected to them.

Bucket List Tip

Invite another couple to join you on these adventures!
Create memories with your closest friends!

17. Escape together

Go to an escape room.

 **Conversation
Starters**

- If you were in a witness protection program, what would your new name be and where would you go?
- Would you break the law to save someone you love?
- What's the most useful thing you own?

☐ *We did it! Bucket List Item Complete.*

18. Water-park

Go have fun at a water-park.

**Conversation
Starters**

- Favorite kind of waterslide?
- What's your favorite way to "waste" time?
- Who is your oldest friend? What do you love most about them?

☐ *We did it! Bucket List Item Complete.*

Make sure to take photos and post them on your iHeartUs app. iHeartUs is a free app for couples that we created for you to strengthen your relationship. Studies have shown that looking at photos of your romantic partner can make you feel even more connected to them.

Bucket List Tip

Collaborate to create a playlist of your favorite songs.
Make it the theme music for the day!

19. Rent a "dream" car

Rent you or your partner's "dream" car.

**Conversation
Starters**

- What is more important to you: a great car or a great house. Why?
- What's your favorite season of the year and why?
- What do you bring with you everywhere you go?

☐ *We did it! Bucket List Item Complete.*

20. Dining safari

Have breakfast at home. Have lunch 20+ miles away. Have dinner 40 + miles away.

Conversation Starters

- If you opened your own business, what would it be?
- What is a controversial opinion you have?
- Who has had the biggest impact on the person you've become?

We did it! Bucket List Item Complete.

Make sure to take photos and post them on your iHeartUs app. iHeartUs is a free app for couples that we created for you to strengthen your relationship. Studies have shown that looking at photos of your romantic partner can make you feel even more connected to them.

Chilllax

/chil·lax | \ chi-'laks/

To calm down, to make less tense.

Bucket List Tip

Cover your person in sticky notes that say what you love about them!

01. Sleep in

Plan to spend all morning in bed together and don't let one another up until noon. Alternative: plan for pillow talk at least an hour before bed.

Conversation Starters

- If you had to choose between staying in bed for 24 hours or staying awake for 24 hours without sleep, what would you choose?
- What is one topic you love to have conversations about? When did you first find out about sex? Who told you?
- Be vulnerable. Share with each other about a time in your life you were really frightened and why.

☐ *We did it! Bucket List Item Complete.*

02. Breakfast in bed

Make your partner breakfast in bed.
Alternative: take your partner out for a surprise breakfast

Conversation Starters

- What are some things that would make your day better if you were having a bad day?
- What is the luckiest thing you've experienced?
- In the next 5-10 years, what are you most looking forward to?

☐ *We did it! Bucket List Item Complete.*

Make sure to take photos and post them on your iHeartUs app. iHeartUs is a free app for couples that we created for you to strengthen your relationship. Studies have shown that looking at photos of your romantic partner can make you feel even more connected to them.

Bucket List Tip

Take a risk and try a new food with these dates! New experiences are more fun together

03. Read together

Go to a bookstore. Read aloud to each other from your favorite books. Or be inspired. Alternative: Watch a TED talk or sermon together or read a self- development or couples book together.

Conversation Starters

- Who inspires you and why?
- Have you ever spoken in front of a large group of people? How was it?
- What book has influenced you the most?

☐ *We did it! Bucket List Item Complete.*

04. Picnic

Go to the grocery store and buy ingredients for a picnic (wine, cheese, French bread; grapes, fruit, rotisserie chicken, etc.) and go to a park or forest for a relaxing picnic date. Don't forget the blanket for some cuddle time.

Conversation Starters

- What do you do to make yourself feel better when you're in a bad mood?
- What smell brings back great memories?
- What was the best time period of your life so far?

We did it! Bucket List Item Complete.

Make sure to take photos and post them on your iHeartUs app. iHeartUs is a free app for couples that we created for you to strengthen your relationship. Studies have shown that looking at photos of your romantic partner can make you feel even more connected to them.

05. Aquarium or zoo visit

Head to the aquarium (or zoo).

Conversation Starters

- What animal or insect do you wish humans could eradicate?
- What animal would be the most annoying if it could talk? What would it sound like?
- What pets did you have while growing up?

☐ *We did it! Bucket List Item Complete.*

06. Laugh together

Go to an improv or comedy show.

Conversation Starters

- What is one of your funniest memories?
- What's the strangest date you've ever been on?
- What crazy thing do you want to try someday?

☐ *We did it! Bucket List Item Complete.*

07. Brunch buddies

After agreeing to sleep in, plan a relaxed weekend brunch date.

Conversation Starters

- If you opened a restaurant what kind of food would you serve?
- What was your favorite food as a kid?
- If you could choose what time you woke up every day, work not being a factor, what time would you want to wake up?

☐ *We did it! Bucket List Item Complete.*

Make sure to take photos and post them on your iHeartUs app. iHeartUs is a free app for couples that we created for you to strengthen your relationship. Studies have shown that looking at photos of your romantic partner can make you feel even more connected to them.

08. Dinner for Two

Find a new and exciting recipe and prepare a meal together. Make a trip to the store to gather the perfect ingredients together.

Conversation Starters

- What is your least favorite food?
- If you could only eat one food, what would you choose?
- What food brings back memories?

☐ *We did it! Bucket List Item Complete.*

09. Take a class together

This could be a ballroom dancing class or learning a new language. Pick the local language of a place you'd like to visit together some day. To practice, try talking to each other using the new language. Choose a watercolor or painting class if you want to explore art; a paint and sip class, a pottery class. The options are endless.

Conversation Starters

- What three words best describe you?
- What art form do you enjoy practicing most? Why?
- What kind of student were you in school?

☐ *We did it! Bucket List Item Complete.*

Make sure to take photos and post them on your iHeartUs app. iHeartUs is a free app for couples that we created for you to strengthen your relationship. Studies have shown that looking at photos of your romantic partner can make you feel even more connected to them.

Bucket List Tip

Choose the outfits you love to see your person in most. Wear those out!

10. Go bowling!

**Bowling is an old-school date idea
with a casual, relaxed feel.**

**Conversation
Starters**

- What is a job you would be horrible at? Why?
- What tradition would you want to pass onto your kids?
- What is your favorite holiday memory?

☐ *We did it! Bucket List Item Complete.*

11. Museum visit

Go to a museum together. Nearly everyone has a museum or several within driving distance. Plan an afternoon wandering around the exhibits. If art isn't your thing, try a history, sport, or cultural museum.

Conversation Starters

- What is a new hobby you would like to try?
- What is another career you think you would love?
- If you gave money to charity, which one would you give to and why? Or towards what cause?

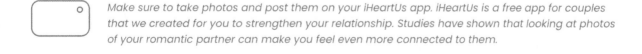

☐ *We did it! Bucket List Item Complete.*

Make sure to take photos and post them on your iHeartUs app. iHeartUs is a free app for couples that we created for you to strengthen your relationship. Studies have shown that looking at photos of your romantic partner can make you feel even more connected to them.

12. Game night

Have couple friends over for a game night.

**Conversation
Starters**

- Would you have dinner with your favorite celebrity or would you rather choose to be a contestant on your favorite game show?
- What are some of the things on your personal bucket list?
- Who is the greatest superhero in your opinion?

☐ *We did it! Bucket List Item Complete.*

13. Play photographer

Set out to explore your town or a special place through a "photographers" eye. It's amazing what details you'll discover that you've never noticed before when you're looking through the lens of a camera! You can also take photos of each other, which will be a romantic way to notice each other in a new way.

Conversation Starters

- Where was the most interesting place you've been? What was unique or interesting about it?
- What is something worth spending more on to get the best?
- What is the most touching or heartwarming thing you've ever seen?

☐ *We did it! Bucket List Item Complete.*

Make sure to take photos and post them on your iHeartUs app. iHeartUs is a free app for couples that we created for you to strengthen your relationship. Studies have shown that looking at photos of your romantic partner can make you feel even more connected to them.

14. Fly kites together

**Fly kites. Stop at the toy store to pick up
a few goodies. Try a Frisbee or a kite for
some outdoor fun.**

Conversation Starters

- What was your favorite cartoon or tv show as a child?
- What was the last funny video you saw? (Show it to them.)
- What do you do to help you de-stress?

☐ *We did it! Bucket List Item Complete.*

Make sure to take photos and post them on your iHeartUs app. iHeartUs is a free app for couples that we created for you to strengthen your relationship. Studies have shown that looking at photos of your romantic partner can make you feel even more connected to them.

15. Random event

Look up a list of events in your area and randomly choose one to attend.

 Conversation Starters

- Why did you decide to do the work you're doing now?
- What are you interested in that most people haven't heard of?
- When do you feel or have you felt most "alive?"

☐ *We did it! Bucket List Item Complete.*

16. Movie night

Plan a movie night together where you watch one of your partner's favorites and one of yours. (You could even cook them their favorite meal.) Alternative: Cheese and wine in front of your favorite romantic comedy movie

Conversation Starters

- Which movie had an impact on you emotionally? Why?
- If you could have been an actor in any movie, which one would it have been? Why?
- What movie universe would you most like to live in?

☐ *We did it! Bucket List Item Complete.*

 Make sure to take photos and post them on your iHeartUs app. iHeartUs is a free app for couples that we created for you to strengthen your relationship. Studies have shown that looking at photos of your romantic partner can make you feel even more connected to them.

Bucket List Tip

Why not take a instant camera with you?
Instant fun and you get to take a memory with you when you go home.

17. Happy hour at home

Buy all the ingredients for your partner's favorite cocktail or craft beer, light the candles and have a romantic, relaxed happy hour before dinner.

Conversation Starters

- What is something considered a luxury that's more like a basic necessity to you that you couldn't live without?
- If you were cryogenically frozen for 100 years, what would your first question be?
- If you could build a house and have unlimited funds to do it, what would it be like?

☐ *We did it! Bucket List Item Complete.*

18. Spa Day

**Plan a spa day for just the two of you.
Or schedule a couple's massage.**

**Conversation
Starters**

- What makes a good life?
- What do you take for granted?
- What are some of your favorite ways to relax?

<!-- checkbox --> We did it! Bucket List Item Complete.

 Make sure to take photos and post them on your iHeartUs app. iHeartUs is a free app for couples that we created for you to strengthen your relationship. Studies have shown that looking at photos of your romantic partner can make you feel even more connected to them.

19. Art & Craft

Pick an art and craft project to do together. You could choose something to beautify your home. Find areas in your home that need to be improved, and work together to make them beautiful.

 Conversation Starters

- If you could create or build anything (business, church, building, non-profit), what would it be?
- What do you want to be remembered for?
- If your life was a book what would the title be?

☐ *We did it! Bucket List Item Complete.*

20. Bingo!

Hit up a Bingo night.

**Conversation
Starters**

- What do you like most about your life right now?
- What is the most immature thing you do?
- What is one of the most memorable gifts you've received?

We did it! Bucket List Item Complete.

Make sure to take photos and post them on your iHeartUs app. iHeartUs is a free app for couples that we created for you to strengthen your relationship. Studies have shown that looking at photos of your romantic partner can make you feel even more connected to them.

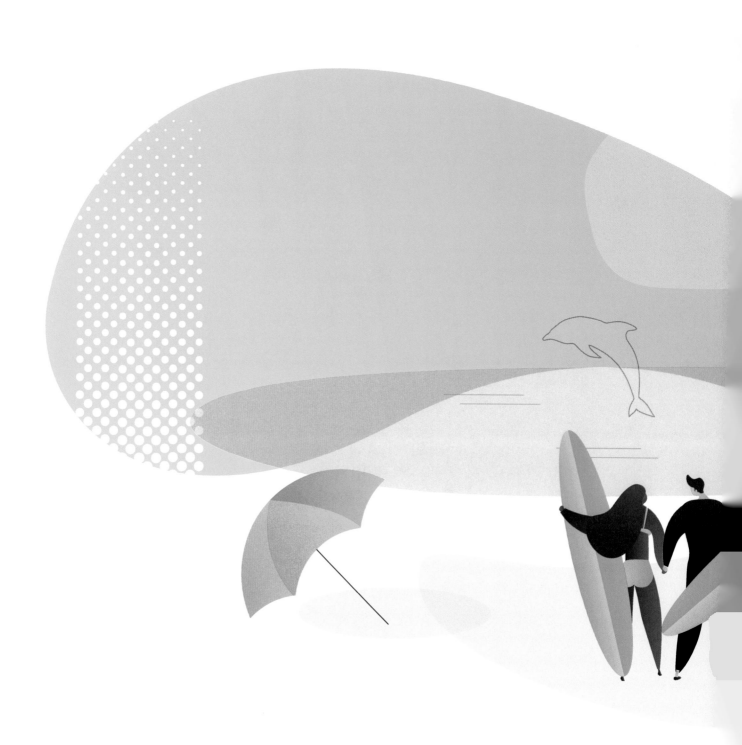

Active

/ˈaktiv/

Engaging or ready to engage in
physically energetic pursuits.

01. Driving range

Practice at the driving range.

**Conversation
Starters**

- When was the first time you hit a golf ball well? How did it feel?
- What is your favorite sport to play?
- What sport would you love to play professionally?

☐ *We did it! Bucket List Item Complete.*

02. Smash rooms

Smash rooms are places that sound exactly like their name. You can go smash things together, get some anger or stress out, and build a great memory!

Conversation Starters

- When is a time you have been the most angry?
- What helps you to de-stress?
- When is a time you have been most proud of how you handled a difficult situation?

 We did it! Bucket List Item Complete.

Make sure to take photos and post them on your iHeartUs app. iHeartUs is a free app for couples that we created for you to strengthen your relationship. Studies have shown that looking at photos of your romantic partner can make you feel even more connected to them.

03. Salsa dancing

Take a salsa dancing class together.

**Conversation
Starters**

- Who taught you how to dance?
- When have you felt the most uninhibited?
- If you could do anything and be guaranteed to succeed, what would you do?

☐ *We did it! Bucket List Item Complete.*

04. Go to an arcade

Who doesn't love a good arcade?

**Conversation
Starters**

- What is one of your favorite childhood memories?
- What makes you feel like a kid all over again?
- What's your favorite candy?

☐ *We did it! Bucket List Item Complete.*

 Make sure to take photos and post them on your iHeartUs app. iHeartUs is a free app for couples that we created for you to strengthen your relationship. Studies have shown that looking at photos of your romantic partner can make you feel even more connected to them.

05. Rooftop pool

Find a rooftop pool and go swimming.

**Conversation
Starters**

- Where is the most relaxing place you've ever been?
- What is one thing you like to do the old-fashioned way?
- What is something everyone should do once in their lives?

☐ *We did it! Bucket List Item Complete.*

Make sure to take photos and post them on your iHeartUs app. iHeartUs is a free app for couples that we created for you to strengthen your relationship. Studies have shown that looking at photos of your romantic partner can make you feel even more connected to them.

06. Caving

Go explore caverns or go spelunking.

**Conversation
Starters**

- When was a time you went exploring?
- Have you ever felt claustrophobic? When?
- When was a time you pushed past your physical limitations and dug deep?

☐ *We did it! Bucket List Item Complete.*

07. Sports tickets

Buy your partner tickets to their favorite sporting event.

Conversation Starters

- What do you like/ not like about participating in sports?
- When did you fall in love with your favorite team?
- Why are you a fan of your favorite team?

☐ *We did it! Bucket List Item Complete.*

Make sure to take photos and post them on your iHeartUs app. iHeartUs is a free app for couples that we created for you to strengthen your relationship. Studies have shown that looking at photos of your romantic partner can make you feel even more connected to them.

08. Run together

Sign up for a color run or mud run or a 5k run in your city.

Conversation Starters

- What is your favorite type of running? Sprint, 5k, half-marathon, marathon, mud run, etc.
- Where is your favorite place to run? Beach, trails, treadmill, etc.
- What do you love or hate the most about running?

☐ *We did it! Bucket List Item Complete.*

09. Ice-skating

Go ice-skating.

**Conversation
Starters**

- What type of skating did you like best as a child?
- What was your worst injury as a kid?
- Would you rather be cold or hot? Why?

☐ *We did it! Bucket List Item Complete.*

Make sure to take photos and post them on your iHeartUs app. iHeartUs is a free app for couples that we created for you to strengthen your relationship. Studies have shown that looking at photos of your romantic partner can make you feel even more connected to them.

10. Rent an ATV

Rent an all terrain vehicle and go have an adventure!

Conversation Starters

- Do you like to take risks and go extremely fast or would you rather take a little risk and go more of an average speed or do you like to play it safe?
- What's the farthest you've ever been from home?
- Are you usually early or late?

☐ *We did it! Bucket List Item Complete.*

11. Play a sport

Play tennis or a new sport together.

**Conversation
Starters**

- What is the best way to start the day?
- What do you want to know more about?
- How many times per week is your ideal playing time for your favorite sport?

☐ *We did it! Bucket List Item Complete.*

Make sure to take photos and post them on your iHeartUs app. iHeartUs is a free app for couples that we created for you to strengthen your relationship. Studies have shown that looking at photos of your romantic partner can make you feel even more connected to them.

12. Share your hobbies

Pick one of your partner's favorite hobbies and do it together.

Conversation Starters

- What was your very first hobby?
- What do you regret not starting when you were younger?
- They say everyone has a book in them. What would yours be about?

☐ *We did it! Bucket List Item Complete.*

13. Work-out together

Take a fun work-out class or try something new and trendy like Crossfit or SurfSet or a spinning class.

Conversation Starters

- What is your favorite type of way to work out?
- What do you love most about exercise?
- If you were put into solitary confinement for 6 months, what would you do to stay sane?

☐ *We did it! Bucket List Item Complete.*

Make sure to take photos and post them on your iHeartUs app. iHeartUs is a free app for couples that we created for you to strengthen your relationship. Studies have shown that looking at photos of your romantic partner can make you feel even more connected to them.

14. Water-sports

Rent a tandem kayak or stand up paddle boards.

**Conversation
Starters**

- If you could have a video of any one event in your life which one would you choose?
- What's one thing you really want but aren't sure you can afford?
- What is one of your funniest memories associated with being in or on the water?

☐ *We did it! Bucket List Item Complete.*

15. Tandem bicycle

Rent a tandem bicycle.

**Conversation
Starters**

- If you could ride a bike anywhere, where would it be?
- What is your preferred mode of transport?
- If you could buy your dream car, what would it be?

☐ *We did it! Bucket List Item Complete.*

16. Rock-climb

Go rock-climbing.

**Conversation
Starters**

- Are you afraid of heights? If not, what is your biggest fear?
- What skill would you like to master?
- What do you wish you knew more about?

☐ *We did it! Bucket List Item Complete.*

Make sure to take photos and post them on your iHeartUs app. iHeartUs is a free app for couples that we created for you to strengthen your relationship. Studies have shown that looking at photos of your romantic partner can make you feel even more connected to them.

17. Treasure-hunting

Go treasure-hunting through geo-caching or to the shooting range.

**Conversation
Starters**

- What do you think about gun laws?
- What do you consider to be your best find?
- Who is a person in your life who has been a gift to you?

☐ *We did it! Bucket List Item Complete.*

18. Snowboarding

Get away for a romantic ski or snowboard weekend.

Conversation Starters

- When was the first time you learned to ski/snowboard?
- What is your most embarrassing moment that happened playing a sport?
- What are some things you've had to unlearn or an area of greatest personal growth?

☐ *We did it! Bucket List Item Complete.*

 Make sure to take photos and post them on your iHeartUs app. iHeartUs is a free app for couples that we created for you to strengthen your relationship. Studies have shown that looking at photos of your romantic partner can make you feel even more connected to them.

Bucket List Tip

Make it a goal to talk to some strangers and make a new friend!

19. Zip-lining

Zip-lining or obstacle course.
Alternative: Break a sweat together—at the gym.

Conversation Starters

- When was the last time you climbed a tree?
- What takes up too much of your time?
- What state or country do you never want to go back to?

☐ *We did it! Bucket List Item Complete.*

20. Mini or frisbee golf

Mini-golf or Frisbee golf (try it blindfolded if you're up for something different). Topgolf, laser tag, or an indoor trampoline park.

Conversation Starters

- What gets you fired up?
- What's the best thing about you?
- What was the best thing about being a kid?

☐ *We did it! Bucket List Item Complete.*

Make sure to take photos and post them on your iHeartUs app. iHeartUs is a free app for couples that we created for you to strengthen your relationship. Studies have shown that looking at photos of your romantic partner can make you feel even more connected to them.

Nature

/ˈnāCHər/

The phenomena of the physical world
collectively, including plants, animals,
the landscape.

01. Go hiking

Hike in the nearest forest.

**Conversation
Starters**

- What is your favorite place in the world?
- What is one of the most beautiful places you've been?
- What is the hardest hike or exercise you've ever done?

☐ *We did it! Bucket List Item Complete.*

02. Ride bikes together

Go for a bike ride together in the neighborhood (or go mountain biking).

Conversation Starters

- Would you rather be driving, biking, boating, kayaking, or on a motorcycle? Why?
- How old were you when you learned to ride a bike? What do you remember about it?
- Were you ever really scared in a moving vehicle? What happened?

☐ *We did it! Bucket List Item Complete.*

Make sure to take photos and post them on your iHeartUs app. iHeartUs is a free app for couples that we created for you to strengthen your relationship. Studies have shown that looking at photos of your romantic partner can make you feel even more connected to them.

03. Bird-watching

Go bird-watching. Sometimes the most romantic activities involve being outdoors together. Check if your favorite local park offers birdwatching tours, or just hang out in nature with binoculars.

 **Conversation Starters**

- What is your favorite animal?
- What is the best pet you've ever had and why?
- How do you feel about hunting as a sport?

☐ *We did it! Bucket List Item Complete.*

04. Berry-picking

Head to the nearest berry farm to go berry-picking.

**Conversation
Starters**

- What is one food that brings back strong memories?
- What's your favorite dessert?
- Do you prefer being active on your day off or just hanging out and relaxing?

We did it! Bucket List Item Complete.

Make sure to take photos and post them on your iHeartUs app. iHeartUs is a free app for couples that we created for you to strengthen your relationship. Studies have shown that looking at photos of your romantic partner can make you feel even more connected to them.

Bucket List Tip

Make it a tech-free day. Ditch the phones until it's time to take that picture!

05. Read in nature

Go to a beautiful place in nature and read together. Author Gary Chapman's book The Five Love Languages is a great book for couples to read together.

Conversation Starters

- If you read The Five Love Languages book, what are your love languages?
- Discuss how you can use those love languages to love each other better.
- In what way are you and your spouse alike? How are you different? Do you think opposites attract?

☐ *We did it! Bucket List Item Complete.*

Make sure to take photos and post them on your iHeartUs app. iHeartUs is a free app for couples that we created for you to strengthen your relationship. Studies have shown that looking at photos of your romantic partner can make you feel even more connected to them.

06. Watch the sunset

**Go somewhere where you can watch the sunset.
(A bottle of wine can't hurt.)**

**Conversation
Starters**

- If your personality had intro music, what song would it be and why?
- What's your favorite thing to do with friends?
- What movie could you watch over and over?

☐ *We did it! Bucket List Item Complete.*

07. Apple picking

Go apple picking at a local orchard.

Conversation Starters

- If you could wear only comfortable or only fashionable clothing every day of your life, which would you choose?
- If you could go on a cross country road trip with someone famous, who would it be?
- If you could sum up the internet in one word what would you say?

 We did it! Bucket List Item Complete.

Make sure to take photos and post them on your iHeartUs app. iHeartUs is a free app for couples that we created for you to strengthen your relationship. Studies have shown that looking at photos of your romantic partner can make you feel even more connected to them.

08. Camp together

Camping together or just camp in your backyard if you want to be spontaneous but comfortable.

 Conversation Starters

- Where do you see yourself living when you retire?
- Where have you travelled and felt most out of place?
- Aside from tv, what's your favorite indoor activity?

☐ *We did it! Bucket List Item Complete.*

09. Boat or canoe

Rent a paddle boat or canoe or go sailing.

Conversation Starters

- If you could have an all-expenses paid trip to any world monument what would it be?
- Would you rather travel every day of your life or never?
- What one job can computers never replace?

☐ *We did it! Bucket List Item Complete.*

Make sure to take photos and post them on your iHeartUs app. iHeartUs is a free app for couples that we created for you to strengthen your relationship. Studies have shown that looking at photos of your romantic partner can make you feel even more connected to them.

10. Go glamping

Go glamping. Choose a place with resort amenities and treat yourselves.

Conversation Starters

- What book or movie describes your life together?
- What actor or actress would play each of you?
- What would the title of the movie or book about your life separate and your life together be called?

☐ *We did it! Bucket List Item Complete.*

11. Botanical garden

Visit a local botanical garden

**Conversation
Starters**

- What is your favorite plant in the garden? Why?
- What's a small detail about your spouse that you love?
- What is something about your partner that no one else (or very few people) know?

☐ *We did it! Bucket List Item Complete.*

 Make sure to take photos and post them on your iHeartUs app. iHeartUs is a free app for couples that we created for you to strengthen your relationship. Studies have shown that looking at photos of your romantic partner can make you feel even more connected to them.

Bucket List Tip

Why not take a instant camera with you?
Instant fun and you get to take a memory with you when you go home.

12. Eat in nature

Go for a drive to a cafe or restaurant that is surrounded by nature (or one that has a great view).

Conversation Starters

- If you could open your own restaurant, what would it be like?
- What was your favorite restaurant to go to as a child, and currently? How has your taste in food changed?
- What's your favorite type of outdoor scenery? Why? Is there a specific memory associated with that kind of place?

☐ *We did it! Bucket List Item Complete.*

13. Playground fun

Play on the playground together and talk about your favorite childhood memories.

**Conversation
Starters**

- Describe one of your most embarrassing moments from your childhood?
- If you could go back and make a certain decision differently, what would it be?
- What are your top 3 hopes and dreams for your children or future children?

☐ *We did it! Bucket List Item Complete.*

Make sure to take photos and post them on your iHeartUs app. iHeartUs is a free app for couples that we created for you to strengthen your relationship. Studies have shown that looking at photos of your romantic partner can make you feel even more connected to them.

14. Go fishing

Go fishing in a beautiful spot.

Conversation Starters

- What traditions do you like the most?
- Describe a time as a child you felt really special or important.
- What is one of your favorite activities that involves a type of animal?

We did it! Bucket List Item Complete.

Bucket List Tip

Collaborate to create a new tradition while you're out!

15. Outdoor concert

Go to an outdoor concert.

**Conversation
Starters**

- Name five things you're thankful for today.
- Do you think we laugh and enjoy life enough together? How can we make more time for fun in our routine?
- What discourages you and slows you down in life or work?

☐ *We did it! Bucket List Item Complete.*

16. Plane-Watching

Chill out together while watching planes land at a place near your local airport. Bring some food so you will have something to munch on while enjoying the sight of landing planes.

Conversation Starters

- Would you rather learn something by reading about it, listening to an explanation, or by hands-on practice? Why?
- If you could take a class on any subject, what would it be?
- If you could teach a class on any skill or subject, what would it be?

☐ *We did it! Bucket List Item Complete.*

Make sure to take photos and post them on your iHeartUs app. iHeartUs is a free app for couples that we created for you to strengthen your relationship. Studies have shown that looking at photos of your romantic partner can make you feel even more connected to them.

17. Batting cages

Engage in some friendly outdoor competition – have a date at batting cages.

Conversation Starters

- What is the best Christmas or birthday gift you've ever received?
- What can we do to make the holidays more meaningful this year?
- If you could have superpowers, what would they be?

☐ *We did it! Bucket List Item Complete.*

18. Dinner Cruise

Whether you live by the ocean or near a lake, you can easily find dinner cruises. Brunch or moonlight cruises are also another good option.

Conversation Starters

- What are the ways that you have grown and changed in the last year? Name positive change in each other.
- Do you enjoy being on or around water? Why or why not?
- What is your favorite season, and why?

 *We did it! Bucket List Item Complete.*

 Make sure to take photos and post them on your iHeartUs app. iHeartUs is a free app for couples that we created for you to strengthen your relationship. Studies have shown that looking at photos of your romantic partner can make you feel even more connected to them.

19. Treasure Hunt

Create a hunt for your person in and around the house or your town. Together, follow the clues or riddles you've created and surprise them with something they love at the end.

Conversation Starters

- Do you enjoy being surprised?
- What was your favorite birthday party and why?
- Do you think you ever care too much about other people's expectations?

☐ *We did it! Bucket List Item Complete.*

20. Blind-folded activity

Do something with one of you blind-folded. Bake a cake, paint a picture or any other activity that can get a little messy.

Conversation Starters

- Would you say that you enjoy adventure?
- What is one adventure that you have always wanted to go on?
- What vacation would you like to plan together for next year?

☐ *We did it! Bucket List Item Complete.*

Make sure to take photos and post them on your iHeartUs app. iHeartUs is a free app for couples that we created for you to strengthen your relationship. Studies have shown that looking at photos of your romantic partner can make you feel even more connected to them.

Romantic

/rō′man(t)ik/

Conducive to or characterized by the
expression of love, readily demonstrating
feelings of love.

Bucket List Tip

Make it special and buy a new outfit or piece for this date! Surprise your person with your new look!

01. Formal date in the city

Plan a formal date out to the best restaurant in the city just because.

Conversation Starters

- Why did you pick this restaurant?
- What do you love about going to the city?
- What's your favorite memory of being in a big city?

☐ *We did it! Bucket List Item Complete.*

02. Musical/Ballet

Buy your partner tickets to a musical or ballet in the closest city.

Conversation Starters

- Talk about childhood memories with the ballet or seeing a musical. If this is the first time for both of you, then ask each other what you're expecting from the experience.
- What do you like about your spouse's outfit and/or how they dress?
- What is something about your spouse that you wish you had too?

☐ *We did it! Bucket List Item Complete.*

 Make sure to take photos and post them on your iHeartUs app. iHeartUs is a free app for couples that we created for you to strengthen your relationship. Studies have shown that looking at photos of your romantic partner can make you feel even more connected to them.

03. Go for a walk

Go for a walk together in a beautiful place.

Conversation Starters

- What do you like about being in nature?
- What's your favorite memory of being silly in a moment you were supposed to be serious?
- What kinds of things do you consider to be romantic?

☐ *We did it! Bucket List Item Complete.*

04. Book a hotel

Splurge on a fancy or boutique hotel room. Make a date for sex.

Conversation Starters

- What gives you butterflies?
- List 3 things you love about your spouse's appearance.
- What makes you feel desired?

We did it! Bucket List Item Complete.

Make sure to take photos and post them on your iHeartUs app. iHeartUs is a free app for couples that we created for you to strengthen your relationship. Studies have shown that looking at photos of your romantic partner can make you feel even more connected to them.

05. Wine tasting

Plan for a day of wine-tasting.

Conversation Starters

- How would you describe our relationship?
- What is your funniest memory from one of our dates?
- What's the best alcoholic beverage you've ever tasted?

☐ *We did it! Bucket List Item Complete.*

06. Your first date, again

Recreate the first date you ever had together.

**Conversation
Starters**

- How did you feel about me on our first date?
- What made you ask me on a date or what made you say yes?
- Why did you choose this first date place?

☐ *We did it! Bucket List Item Complete.*

07. Go dancing

Hit the club and dance together.

**Conversation
Starters**

- Ask each other how dancing makes them feel (make each other feel comfortable as well as take a fun risk together).
- What do you find sexy about your spouse when they dance?
- What is your favorite song to dance to?

We did it! Bucket List Item Complete.

 Make sure to take photos and post them on your iHeartUs app. iHeartUs is a free app for couples that we created for you to strengthen your relationship. Studies have shown that looking at photos of your romantic partner can make you feel even more connected to them.

08. Surprise dinner party

Plan a surprise dinner party with your closest couple friends.

Conversation Starters

- Have each couple say something they love about their spouse in front of everyone.
- What was your favorite date together? Have everyone share.
- Share a funny date story.

☐ *We did it! Bucket List Item Complete.*

09. Massage each other

Exchange massages.

**Conversation
Starters**

- What is your idea of a fulfilling sex life?
- What makes someone a good listener?
- What kind of physical touch do you enjoy most?

We did it! Bucket List Item Complete.

Make sure to take photos and post them on your iHeartUs app. iHeartUs is a free app for couples that we created for you to strengthen your relationship. Studies have shown that looking at photos of your romantic partner can make you feel even more connected to them.

10. Jazz evening out

Go to a jazz club together.

**Conversation
Starters**

- What's your favorite style of music? Has it changed over the years?
- What's your favorite song on the radio currently?
- In what way(s) does music affect you?

☐ *We did it! Bucket List Item Complete.*

11. Time Capsule

Collect favorite pictures, momentos and items that hold memories from the year. Dream together and write down aspirations for the upcoming year and include them! Place these in a box, seal it with plastic and bury it. Set a reminder to open up the box in 1 year.

Conversation Starters

- If you could travel back in time, what memory would you go back to?
- Do you think our schedules are too busy? How can we simplify it if so?
- Describe your idea of a perfect day together. When can you make that happen

☐ *We did it! Bucket List Item Complete.*

Make sure to take photos and post them on your iHeartUs app. iHeartUs is a free app for couples that we created for you to strengthen your relationship. Studies have shown that looking at photos of your romantic partner can make you feel even more connected to them.

Bucket List Tip

Write each other short notes in the morning about your favorite memory of them. Exchange the notes at the end of the adventure!

12. Horse-drawn carriage

Take a horse-drawn carriage ride.

Conversation Starters

- Share some memories of your wedding day. What emotions were you feeling? What part of the ceremony stands out in your mind? (If you're not married yet, share some dreams of your future wedding day.)
- How can we be more intentionally romantic with each other?
- Name 3 things that make a relationship successful. Are we doing those things?

☐ *We did it! Bucket List Item Complete.*

13. Surprise Trip

Plan a surprise overnight trip.

Conversation Starters

- Where is the most beautiful, awe-inspiring place you've been?
- What would be your perfect weekend?
- Where would you like to travel to if you could go anywhere?

We did it! Bucket List Item Complete.

Make sure to take photos and post them on your iHeartUs app. iHeartUs is a free app for couples that we created for you to strengthen your relationship. Studies have shown that looking at photos of your romantic partner can make you feel even more connected to them.

14. Stargaze

Stargaze or go to the local planetarium.

**Conversation
Starters**

- Describe your dream house? Where would it be?
- What are 3 things I do that make you feel special and loved?
- What first attracted you to me?

☐ *We did it! Bucket List Item Complete.*

Make sure to take photos and post them on your iHeartUs app. iHeartUs is a free app for couples that we created for you to strengthen your relationship. Studies have shown that looking at photos of your romantic partner can make you feel even more connected to them.

15. Couple shoot

Ask a friend who's good at photography to do a couples photo shoot for you in a beautiful location.

Conversation Starters

- Ask each other how they feel about taking pictures (If your spouse is uncomfortable, how can you help each other?).
- Talk about your favorite pictures you've taken together and where they were.
- What's the worst picture you've ever seen of yourself?

☐ *We did it! Bucket List Item Complete.*

16. Book a Cruise

Cruise vacations have activities for everyone.

Conversation Starters

- What do you like to do to relax on vacation?
- Where would you go if you could go on a cruise anywhere just the two of you?
- Would you rather stay busy doing fun activities or adventures on vacation or would you rather hang out at the beach and do nothing?

☐ *We did it! Bucket List Item Complete.*

Make sure to take photos and post them on your iHeartUs app. iHeartUs is a free app for couples that we created for you to strengthen your relationship. Studies have shown that looking at photos of your romantic partner can make you feel even more connected to them.

Bucket List Tip

Turn up the romance! Add in some candles, flowers and wine for these at-home dates.

17. Fancy night in

Create a surprise "Fancy Night In."

Conversation Starters

- Tell each other the first thing that drew you to your spouse.
- What was your favorite fancy date together and why?
- When do you feel most cherished by your spouse?

We did it! Bucket List Item Complete.

18. Movies at home

Watch one of the first movies you saw together at home. Snuggle up real close.

Conversation Starters

- What is your favorite movie snack from your childhood?
- Would you rather go out to the movie theatre or watch one at home?
- What's one of your all-time favorite films?

☐ *We did it! Bucket List Item Complete.*

Make sure to take photos and post them on your iHeartUs app. iHeartUs is a free app for couples that we created for you to strengthen your relationship. Studies have shown that looking at photos of your romantic partner can make you feel even more connected to them.

Bucket List Tip

Why not take a instant camera with you?
Instant fun and you get to take a memory with you when you go home.

19. Theatre night

**It's a little classier than a movie and you get to dress up
and soak in some culture.**

**Conversation
Starters**

- What's your earliest memory of getting dressed up?
- What do you enjoy about going to the theater?
- What kind of emotions does it bring up?
- Is there a famous theater or Broadway show that you'd like to see some day?

☐ *We did it! Bucket List Item Complete.*

20. Celebrate each other

Romantic date or the perfect way to celebrate an anniversary: put on a white dress, have him put on a fancy suit and go for a walk in the forest carrying a bouquet of flowers.

Read a love poem or pray together or re-write the vows you would say to one another now at this point, knowing what a committed relationship is about. Commit to loving one another for another year.

Conversation Starters

- What are the main things you love about your partner?
- Is there a specific place you'd like to live some day in the future? Dream like money is no option.
- If you could (or had to) spend 3 days at home together without technology, what would you do?

☐ *We did it! Bucket List Item Complete.*

Make sure to take photos and post them on your iHeartUs app. iHeartUs is a free app for couples that we created for you to strengthen your relationship. Studies have shown that looking at photos of your romantic partner can make you feel even more connected to them.

Made in the USA
San Bernardino, CA
30 June 2020